# THE MAGNIFICENT PRAYERS

of

## Saint Bridget of Sweden

Based on the Passion and Death of
Our Lord and Savior Jesus Christ

Taken from
*The Revelations of Saint Bridget*

*"If any man will come after me, let him deny
himself, and take up his cross, and follow me.
For he that will save his life, shall lose it: and he
that shall lose his life for my sake, shall find it."*
—Matt. 16:24-25

TAN BOOKS AND PUBLISHERS, INC.
Rockford, Illinois 61105

Imprimatur: ✠ V. Germond, Vic. Gen.
Niciae
September 23, 1940

*32nd Printing*

This edition was first published in 1971 by Marian Publications, South Bend, Indiana. First TAN edition published in 1983.

Copyright © 1971 by Marian Publications

Copyright © 1983 by TAN Books and Publishers, Inc.

ISBN 0-89555-220-5

Printed and bound in the United States of America.

*Quantity Discount*

| | | |
|---|---|---|
| 1 copy | 2.00 | |
| 5 copies | 1.25 each | 6.25 total |
| 10 copies | 1.00 each | 10.00 total |
| 25 copies | .80 each | 20.00 total |
| 50 copies | .70 each | 35.00 total |
| 100 copies | .60 each | 60.00 total |
| 500 copies | .50 each | 250.00 total |
| 1,000 copies | .40 each | 400.00 total |

U.S. & CANADIAN POST./HDLG: If total order = $1-$10, add $3.00;
$10.01-$25, add $5.00; $25.01-$50.00, add $6.00;
$50.01-$75, add $7.00; $75.01-$150.00, add $8.00; $150.01-up, add $10.00.

TAN BOOKS AND PUBLISHERS, INC.
P.O. Box 424
Rockford, Illinois 61105
1983

# PUBLISHER'S NOTE

*The Magnificent Prayers* were copied from a book printed in Toulouse in 1740 and published by Father Adrien Parvilliers of the Society of Jesus, Missionary Apostolic of the Holy Land, with the approbation, permission and recommendation to spread the devotion. At the time of St. Bridget in the 14th century, printing had not yet been invented, and books had to be reproduced by copyists. Pope Urban VI encouraged the multiplication of copies of *The Revelations of St. Bridget,* from which these prayers have been taken. Kings, bishops, universities, convents and libraries were clamoring for them.

The books containing these prayers have been approved by a great number of prelates, among them His Eminence Cardinal Giraud of Cambria in 1845 and Archbishop Florian of Toulouse in 1863. *The Revelations of St. Bridget* were blessed by His Holiness Pope Pius IX on May 31, 1862. Finally, they were recommended by the great Congress of Malines on August 22, 1863.

Those who visit the Church of St. Paul in Rome can see the life-size crucifix sculptured by Pietro Cavallini, before which St. Bridget knelt, and there can read the following inscription: *"Pendentis pendente Dei verba accepit aure accipit at verbum corde Brigitta Deum. Anno Jubilei MCCCL,"* which recalls the prodigy of the crucifix conversing with St. Bridget. (Translation: "Bridget not only receives the words of God hanging in the air, but takes the word of God into her heart. Jubilee Year 1350.")

For many years *The Magnificent Prayers* were published with twenty-one promises given to her, according to St. Bridget, by Our Lord, along with the prayers. These promises offered wonderful graces and benefits to those who, for one year, recite the prayers, as well as graces for members of their families. Originally, the prayers were published along with the promises under the title *The Magnificent Promises.* But on January 28, 1954, the

Holy Office in Rome issued a Monitum prohibiting publication of the twenty-one promises. (See *Acta Apostolicae Sedis,* XLVI [1954]:64.) The Holy Office warned that the supernatural origin of the promises has not been proved in any way. No proscription, however, was issued against the prayers themselves. Faithful to that directive, we have here issued *The Magnificent Prayers* without the attending promises. It is our conviction that Our Divine Savior wants us to say these prayers in order to honor His Passion and Death, and that we, for our part, should trust in Him to shower us and those for whom we pray with such graces as He in His tender mercy wants to bestow. The purpose for which these prayers have been printed in this inexpensive format is to promote devotion to the Passion of Our Lord, and it is our hope and prayer that the Faithful will circulate them widely, realizing—as *many* saints have deposed—that meditating on the Passion is most efficacious for our own spiritual growth and most pleasing to Our Divine Lord.

The Image of the Holy Face of Jesus
Taken from the Shroud of Turin

# SAINT BRIDGET OF SWEDEN

St. Brigitte or St. Bridget, daughter of Birgir, royal blood prince of Sweden, was born about the year 1302 of highly pious parents. Having lost her virtuous mother soon after birth, little Bridget was brought up by one of her highly virtuous aunts. She could not speak before the age of three, but as soon as she spoke, she began praising God. In early childhood serious discourses pleased her, and grace powerfully filled her heart so that only pious readings attracted her.

At the age of ten she was particularly touched by a sermon she heard on the Passion of Our Lord. The following night she believed that she saw Our Lord nailed to the cross and all covered with blood and wounds. At the same time she heard a voice saying: *"Look upon Me, My daughter."* *"O Dear Lord,"* asked St. Bridget, *"Who has treated You so cruelly?"* Our Lord replied: *"Those who despise Me and are insensible to My love for them."* That mysterious dream left so deep an impression on her that, from then on, she continually meditated on the sufferings of Our Lord Jesus Christ, which drove her to tears.

At the age of 15, through obedience, she was married to Prince Ulf, a very pious young man and they had eight children, and one of her daughters became St. Catherine of Sweden.

St. Bridget's example more than her instructions sanctified her large family. Her revelations and other celestial favors made her all the more fervent and humble. She died at Rome in 1373 after having returned from a pilgrimage to the Holy Land.

She practiced mental prayer and meditated often on the life and sufferings of Our Lord Jesus Christ throughout the year. She founded the Brigittines.

St. Bridget of Sweden (1302 - 1373)

# FIRST PRAYER

*Our Father—Hail Mary*

O Jesus Christ! Eternal Sweetness to those who love Thee, Joy surpassing all joy and all desire, Salvation and Hope of all sinners, Thou Who hast proved that Thou hast no greater desire than to be amongst men, even assuming human nature during the course of time for love of men, recall all the sufferings which Thou hast endured from the first moment of Thy conception, and especially during Thy Passion, as it was decreed and ordained from all eternity in the divine plan.

Remember, O Lord, that during the Last Supper with Thy disciples, having washed their feet, Thou gavest them Thy precious Body and Blood, and while at the same time Thou didst sweetly console them, Thou didst foretell them Thy coming Passion.

Remember the sadness and bitterness Thou didst experience in Thy soul as Thou prayed: "My soul is sorrowful even unto death."

Remember all the fear, anguish, and pain Thou didst suffer in Thy delicate body before the Crucifixion when, after having prayed three separate times, bathed in a sweat of blood, Thou wast betrayed by Judas, Thy disciple, arrested by the people of a nation Thou hadst chosen and elevated, accused by false witnesses, unjustly judged by three judges: all this in the flower of Thy youth and during the solemn Paschal season.

Remember that Thou wast despoiled of Thy garments and clothed with the garments of derision; that Thy face and eyes were veiled; that Thou wast buffeted, crowned with thorns, a scepter placed in Thy hands; that Thou wast fastened to a column and crushed with blows and overwhelmed with affronts and outrages.

In memory of all these pains and sufferings which Thou didst endure before Thy Passion on the cross, grant that before I die, I may make with true contrition a sincere and entire confession, make worthy satisfaction, and be granted the remission of all my sins. Amen.

# SECOND PRAYER

*Our Father—Hail Mary*

O Jesus! True Liberty of Angels, Paradise of Delights, remember the horror and sadness Thou didst endure when Thy enemies, like furious lions, surrounded Thee, and by thousands of blows, insults, lacerations, and other unheard-of cruelties, tormented Thee at will.

Through these torments and insulting words, I beg Thee, O my Savior, to deliver me from all enemies, both visible and invisible; and under Thy protection may I attain the perfection of eternal salvation. Amen.

# THIRD PRAYER

*Our Father—Hail Mary*

O Jesus! Creator of Heaven and Earth, Whom nothing can encompass or limit, Thou Who dost enfold and hold all under Thy loving power, remember the very bitter pain which Thou didst suffer when the Jews nailed Thy sacred hands and feet to the cross by blow after blow with big blunt nails, and, not finding Thee in a pitiable enough state to satisfy their rage, enlarged Thy wounds, and added pain to pain, and with indescribable cruelty stretched Thy body on the cross and dislocated Thy bones by pulling them on all sides. I beg of Thee, O Jesus, by the memory of this most holy and most loving suffering of the cross, grant me the grace to fear Thee and to love Thee. Amen.

# FOURTH PRAYER

*Our Father—Hail Mary*

O Jesus! Heavenly Physician, raised aloft on the cross in order that through Thy wounds ours might be healed, remember the bruises Thou didst suffer and the weakness of all Thy members, which were distended to such a degree that never was there pain like unto Thine. From the crown of Thy head to the soles of Thy feet, there was not one spot on Thy body which was not in torment; and yet, forgetting all Thy sufferings, Thou didst not cease to pray to Thy Heavenly Father for Thy enemies, saying: "Father, forgive them, for they know not what they do."

Through this great mercy, and in memory of this suffering, grant that the remembrance of Thy most bitter Passion may effect in us a perfect contrition and the remission of all our sins. Amen.


# FIFTH PRAYER

*Our Father—Hail Mary*

O Jesus! Mirror of Eternal Splendor, remember the sadness which Thou experienced when, contemplating in the light of Thy Divinity the predestination of those who would be saved by the merits of Thy sacred Passion, Thou didst see at the same time the great multitude of reprobates who would be damned for their sins; and Thou didst complain bitterly of those hopeless, lost, and unfortunate sinners.

Through this abyss of compassion and pity, and especially through the goodness which Thou displayed to the good thief when Thou saidst to him, "This day thou shalt be with Me in Paradise," I beg of Thee, O sweet Jesus, that at the hour of my death, Thou wilt show me mercy. Amen.

## SIXTH PRAYER

*Our Father—Hail Mary*

O Jesus! King most loving and most desirable, remember the grief which Thou didst suffer when, naked and like a common criminal, Thou wast raised and fastened to the cross; when all Thy relatives and friends abandoned Thee, except Thy beloved Mother, who remained close to Thee during Thy agony, and whom Thou didst entrust to Thy faithful disciple when Thou saidst to Mary, "Woman, behold thy son," and to St. John, "Behold thy Mother."

I beg of Thee, O my Savior, by the sword of sorrow which pierced the soul of Thy holy Mother, to have compassion on me in all my afflictions and tribulations, both corporal and spiritual, and to assist me in all my trials, and especially at the hour of my death. Amen.

# SEVENTH PRAYER

*Our Father—Hail Mary*

O Jesus! Inexhaustible Fountain of Compassion, Who by a profound gesture of love said from the cross, "I thirst," and Who suffered from the thirst for the salvation of the human race, I beg of Thee, O my Savior, to inflame in our hearts the desire to tend toward perfection in all our acts, and to extinguish in us the concupiscence of the flesh and the ardor of worldly desires. Amen.

# EIGHTH PRAYER

*Our Father—Hail Mary*

O Jesus! Sweetness of Hearts, Delight of the Spirit, by the bitterness of the gall and vinegar which Thou didst taste on the cross for love of us, grant us the grace to receive worthily Thy precious Body and Blood during our life and at the hour of our death, that It may serve us as a remedy of consolation for our souls. Amen.

## NINTH PRAYER

*Our Father—Hail Mary*

O Jesus! Royal Virtue, Joy of the Mind, recall the pain Thou didst endure when, plunged in the ocean of bitterness at the approach of death, insulted, outraged by the Jews, Thou didst cry out in a loud voice that Thou wast abandoned by Thy Father, saying: "My God, My God, why hast Thou forsaken Me?" Through this anguish, I beg of Thee, O my Savior, not to abandon me in the terrors and pains of my death. Amen.

## TENTH PRAYER

*Our Father—Hail Mary*

O Jesus! Who art the beginning and end of all things, life and virtue, remember that for our sakes Thou wast plunged into an abyss of suffering, from the soles of Thy feet to the crown of Thy head. In consideration of the enormity of Thy wounds, teach me to keep, through pure love, Thy commandments, which are a wide and easy path for those who love Thee. Amen.

# ELEVENTH PRAYER

*Our Father—Hail Mary*

O Jesus! Deep Abyss of Mercy, I beg of Thee, in memory of Thy wounds, which penetrated to the very marrow of Thy bones and to the depth of Thy being, to draw me, a miserable sinner overwhelmed by my offenses, away from sin and to hide me from Thy face, justly irritated against me; hide me in Thy wounds until Thy anger and indignation shall have passed away. Amen.

# TWELFTH PRAYER

*Our Father—Hail Mary*

O Jesus! Mirror of Truth, Symbol of Unity, Link of Charity, remember the multitude of wounds with which Thou wast afflicted from head to foot, torn and reddened by the spilling of Thy adorable blood. O great and universal pain which Thou didst suffer in Thy virginal flesh for love of us! Sweetest Jesus! What is there Thou couldst have done for us which Thou hast not done?

May the fruit of Thy sufferings be renewed in my soul by the faithful remembrance of Thy Passion, and may Thy love increase in my heart each day until I see Thee in eternity, Thou Who art the treasure of every real good and every joy, which I beg Thee to grant me, O sweetest Jesus, in Heaven. Amen.

# THIRTEENTH PRAYER

*Our Father—Hail Mary*

O Jesus! Strong Lion, immortal and invincible King, remember the pain Thou didst endure when all Thy strength, both moral and physical, was entirely exhausted; Thou didst bow Thy head, saying: "It is consummated."

Through this anguish and grief, I beg of Thee, O Lord, have mercy on me at the hour of my death, when my mind will be greatly troubled and my soul will be in anguish. Amen.

# FOURTEENTH PRAYER

*Our Father—Hail Mary*

O Jesus! Only Son of the Father, Splendor and Figure of His Substance, remember the simple and humble recommendation Thou didst make of Thy soul to Thy eternal Father, saying, "Father, into Thy hands I commend My spirit," and when, Thy body all torn and Thy heart broken and the bowels of Thy mercy open to redeem us, Thou didst expire. By this precious death, I beg Thee, O King of Saints, to comfort me and give me help to resist the devil, the flesh, and the world, so that, being dead to the world, I may live for Thee alone. I beg of Thee at the hour of my death to receive me, a pilgrim and an exile, returning to Thee. Amen.

# FIFTEENTH PRAYER

*Our Father—Hail Mary*

O Jesus! True and Fruitful Vine! Remember the abundant outpouring of blood which Thou didst so generously shed, pressed down and running over as the grape crushed in the wine-press.

From Thy side, pierced with a lance by a soldier, blood and water issued forth until there was not left in Thy body a single drop; and finally, like a bundle of myrrh lifted to the very top of the cross, Thy delicate flesh was destroyed, the very substance of Thy body withered, and the marrow of Thy bones dried up.

Through this bitter Passion, and through the outpouring of Thy Precious Blood, I beg of Thee, O sweet Jesus, to pierce my heart, so that my tears of penitence and love may be my bread night and day. May I be converted entirely to Thee; may my heart be Thy perpetual resting-place; may my conversation be pleasing to Thee; and may the end of my life be so praiseworthy that I may merit Heaven, and there with Thy saints praise Thee forever. Amen.

*If you have enjoyed this book, consider making your next selection from among the following . . .*

Prices subject to change.